SCIENCE WORKS!

LIGHT

STEVE PARKER

For a free color catalog describing Gareth Stevens Publishing's list of high-quality books and multimedia programs, call 1-800-542-2595 (USA) or 1-800-461-9120 (Canada). Gareth Stevens Publishing's Fax: (414) 225-0377. See our catalog, too, on the World Wide Web: http://gsinc.com

Library of Congress Cataloging-in-Publication Data

Parker, Steve.
    Light / by Steve Parker; [illustrators . . . Chris Lyons . . . et al.]
      p. cm. — (Science works!)
    Includes index.
    Summary: Text and experiments demonstrate the properties, behavior, and uses of light.
    ISBN 0-8368-1963-2 (lib. bdg.)
    1. Light—Juvenile literature. 2. Light—Experiments—Juvenile literature. [1. Light—Experiments. 2. Experiments.] I. Lyons, Chris, ill. II. Title. III. Series: Parker, Steve. Science works!
QC360.P36   1997
535—dc21   97-10476

First published in North America in 1997 by
Gareth Stevens Publishing
1555 North RiverCenter Drive, Suite 201
Milwaukee, WI 53212 USA

This U.S. edition © 1997 by Gareth Stevens, Inc. Created with original © 1995 by Macdonald Young Books Ltd., Campus 400, Maylands Avenue, Hemel Hempstead, Hertfordshire, England HP2 7EZ. Additional end matter © 1997 by Gareth Stevens, Inc.

Illustrators: Chris Lyons, Martin Woodward, Simone End, Bob Moulder

Printed in Mexico

1 2 3 4 5 6 7 8 9 01 00 99 98 97

SCIENCE WORKS !

LIGHT

STEVE PARKER

Gareth Stevens Publishing
MILWAUKEE

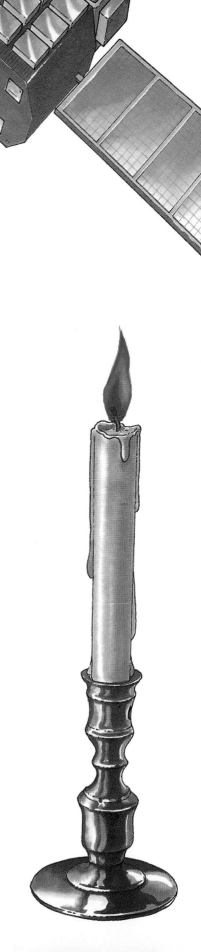

CONTENTS

Words that appear in the glossary are in **boldface** type the first time they occur in the text.

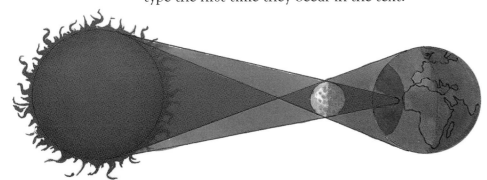

LIGHT

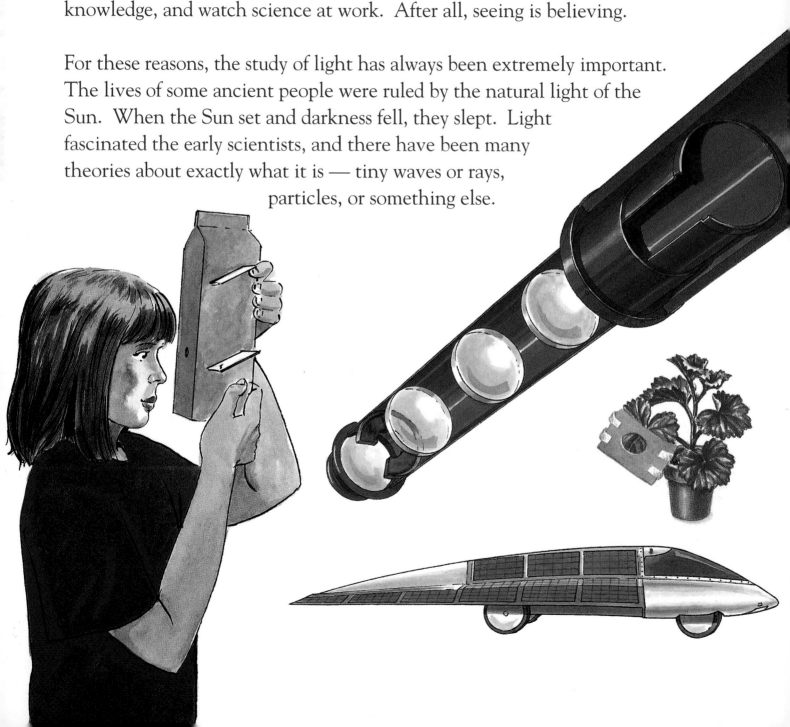

Where would we be without light? Stumbling around in the dark! Most humans rely mainly on sight to discover what is happening around them. Up to two-thirds of the human brain's awareness is taken up by what is seen. Hearing, smell, and the other senses can be thought of as less important. With light to see by, we can find our food and our way, appreciate beauty, take in knowledge, and watch science at work. After all, seeing is believing.

For these reasons, the study of light has always been extremely important. The lives of some ancient people were ruled by the natural light of the Sun. When the Sun set and darkness fell, they slept. Light fascinated the early scientists, and there have been many theories about exactly what it is — tiny waves or rays, particles, or something else.

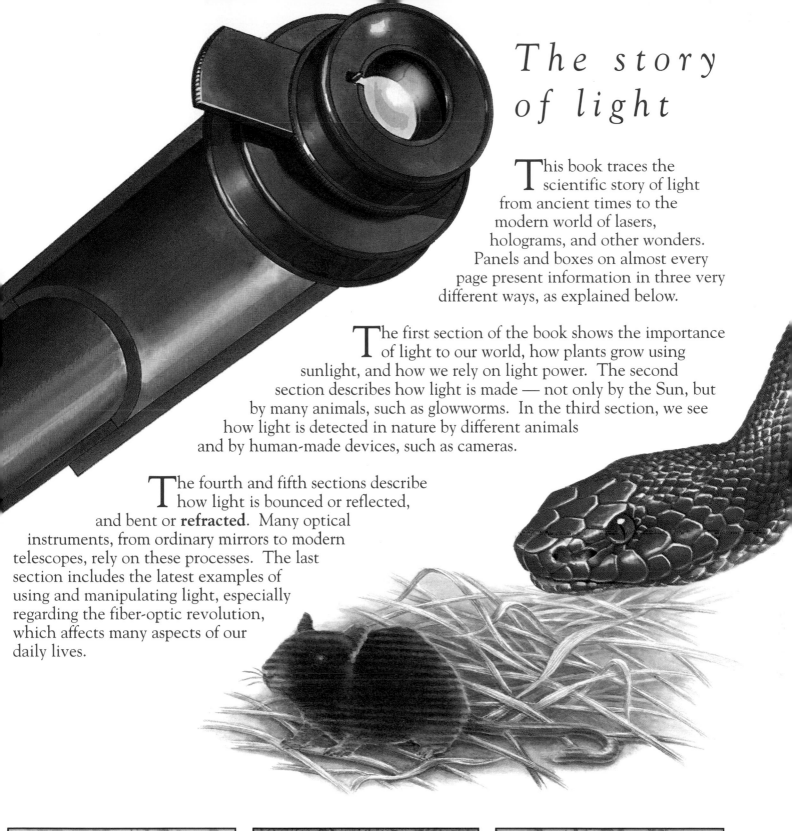

The story of light

This book traces the scientific story of light from ancient times to the modern world of lasers, holograms, and other wonders. Panels and boxes on almost every page present information in three very different ways, as explained below.

The first section of the book shows the importance of light to our world, how plants grow using sunlight, and how we rely on light power. The second section describes how light is made — not only by the Sun, but by many animals, such as glowworms. In the third section, we see how light is detected in nature by different animals and by human-made devices, such as cameras.

The fourth and fifth sections describe how light is bounced or reflected, and bent or **refracted**. Many optical instruments, from ordinary mirrors to modern telescopes, rely on these processes. The last section includes the latest examples of using and manipulating light, especially regarding the fiber-optic revolution, which affects many aspects of our daily lives.

FAMOUS FIRSTS

Knowledge thrives on firsts, such as the first person to discover a scientific law or make an invention. The *Famous Firsts* panels describe these first achievers.

DIY SCIENCE

Follow in the footsteps of well-known scientists by trying the tests and experiments in "Do-It-Yourself" form, using everyday materials, as shown in the *DIY Science* panels.

SPECIAL FX

Scientific processes and principles can have fascinating, even startling, results. The *Special FX* projects show you how to produce these special effects. Most items are readily available in your home.

Natural Light

In the natural world, light is all around. During daytime, the Sun shines and illuminates the scene. As Earth turns and the Sun goes below the horizon, the light fades. But even at night, there is light — from the changing face of the Moon and the twinkling stars to the eerie glow of insects among the trees and fish in the seas.

The Moon orbits our Earth. If the Moon comes between the Earth and the Sun, it blocks the Sun from part of Earth. This is called a solar eclipse.

During a solar eclipse in ancient times, some people worried that the Sun might never return. They prayed and offered gifts and sacrifices to the Sun god.

Many ancient peoples worshiped the Sun as their god or chief spirit. The Sun was seen as a fiery deity that brought light and life.

The edge of the Sun shows as a halo, or corona, around the dark disk of the Moon during a solar eclipse. As the Moon continues its orbit, the Sun is revealed again.

Life would not exist on Earth without light and heat from the Sun. Light lets us see what we are doing and where we are going. Ancient peoples had no electric light bulbs, central heating, or wristwatches. They waited every day for the Sun to rise and bring brightness and warmth to the world. Their clock was the path of the Sun across the sky.

Ancient peoples also knew that the Sun's light and warmth made their crops grow. In fact, light is the basis of food for all creatures because of the way plants use it. Plants trap the energy contained in light through **photosynthesis** (*see opposite*). They do this using **chlorophyll**, a green substance

FASCINATING FACTS

- The Sun is 863,745 miles (1,390,000 kilometers) across, which is over one hundred times Earth's diameter. It is an average of 93 million miles (150 million km) from Earth.

- Of the light, heat, and other energy given out by the Sun, only one-thousandth of one-millionth of it reaches Earth.

- Of the Sun's light, heat, and other energy that reaches Earth, about one-third never reaches the surface. It is reflected back into space by the atmosphere and clouds.

FAMOUS FIRSTS

THE SUNDIAL
The sundial has a central stick or pointer, the gnomon, that casts a shadow. As the Sun travels across the sky, it shines from different directions. The shadow of the gnomon moves, falling on a dial that shows the time. The Babylonians first used sundials over four thousand years ago. However, the sundial is of no use on a cloudy day or at night!

Sundials were often used as church clocks, which were the central point of a village.

This sixteenth-century double-sundial has a pointer on the upright column and one on the front face.

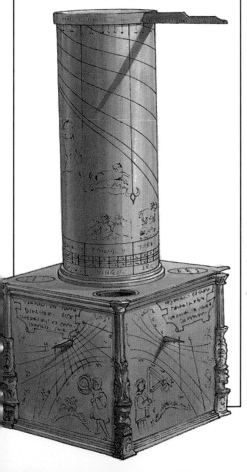

DIY SCIENCE

SUNDIAL TIME
Make a simple sundial, and put it outside on a sunny day. Using a wristwatch, mark the position of the shadow on its dial at each hour. Try the sundial a few weeks later, setting it first thing in the morning. Is it still correct?

You need
Cardboard, scissors, wristwatch, two pencils.

1. Cut out a circle of cardboard, and push a pencil through the middle to make the gnomon. Stick the pencil into the ground in a sunny place.

2. Draw and number the site of the shadow on the dial with a pencil, labeling every hour on the hour as shown by your watch.

3. A few weeks later, put the sundial in the same place. At 9 a.m. twist the dial so the gnomon's shadow falls on the 9 a.m. mark. Check the sundial later. Does the Sun now have a different path? Do you know why?

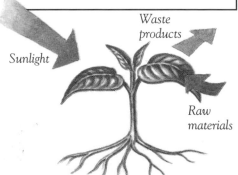

Sunlight

Waste products

Raw materials

SPECIAL FX

LIGHT FOR LIFE
Show that plants need light to live and grow. Block off light to a leaf using black paper and tape. After a few days, the leaf in the dark looks pale since it cannot photosynthesize to get the energy to live. Allow light to reach it again, and the leaf will recover.

You need
A plant, two sheets of black paper, tape.

1. Tape the sheets of paper over one of the large, strong leaves, one sheet on each side.

2. After several days, remove the paper. The leaf beneath is pale and unhealthy because of lack of light.

9

in their leaves. The chlorophyll takes in the energy and converts it into energy-rich chemicals, such as sugars, in the plant's sap. The plant uses this energy to live and grow by making roots, stems, leaves, and flowers.

Herbivorous animals eat plants, taking in the energy-rich chemicals and using them for their own living and growing processes. Carnivorous creatures eat these animals for food, getting energy and growth materials from their flesh.

In this way, the original light energy from the Sun passes first into plants and then into the complicated web of animal foods. In other words, all life on Earth is powered by light energy from the Sun.

At night, ancient peoples were probably fascinated by the light of the stars as the stars seemed to whirl across the sky. They saw the shapes of humans, animals, and various objects in the star patterns. They invented names for them and stories about them. This was the origin of the **constellations** and the signs of the zodiac. Today, there are so many lights on streets and buildings that they blot out much of the natural starlight. In the cities, we are largely strangers to the wonders of the night sky.

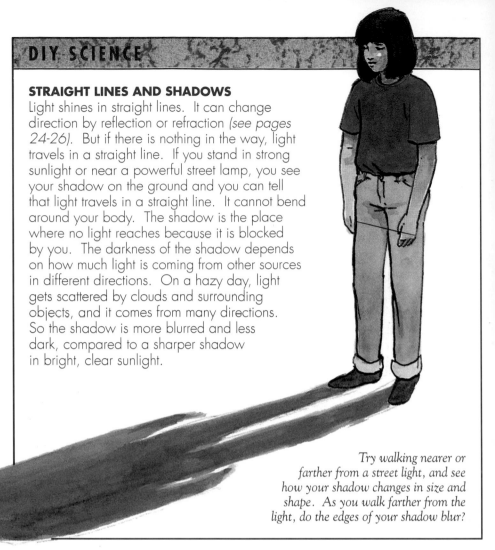

DIY SCIENCE

STRAIGHT LINES AND SHADOWS
Light shines in straight lines. It can change direction by reflection or refraction *(see pages 24-26)*. But if there is nothing in the way, light travels in a straight line. If you stand in strong sunlight or near a powerful street lamp, you see your shadow on the ground and you can tell that light travels in a straight line. It cannot bend around your body. The shadow is the place where no light reaches because it is blocked by you. The darkness of the shadow depends on how much light is coming from other sources in different directions. On a hazy day, light gets scattered by clouds and surrounding objects, and it comes from many directions. So the shadow is more blurred and less dark, compared to a sharper shadow in bright, clear sunlight.

Try walking nearer or farther from a street light, and see how your shadow changes in size and shape. As you walk farther from the light, do the edges of your shadow blur?

DIY SCIENCE

A BRIGHT SPARK
You need
Two pieces of flint rock, thick gloves, protective eye goggles, adult supervision.

Today, we use matches to light a fire. But before there were matches, people used rocks. A type of rock called flint produces sparks when struck. A spark is both light and heat. Pieces of flint were used in cannons and guns of long ago to make the sparks to light the gunpowder. One type of gun was called the flintlock because of flint.

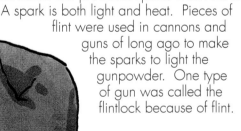

Make sure your hands and eyes are well protected as you strike the flints together. You will notice the sparks best in dim light.

10

STRAIGHT AND CURVED

German astronomer Johannes Kepler (1571-1630) was one of the first scientists to make accurate studies of how light travels in straight lines. He observed the planets and stars with the newly invented telescope.

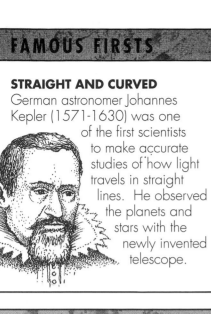

FASCINATING FACTS

- It is not completely true that light always travels in straight lines. If light passes near a huge object, such as a star, it is attracted by the star's immense force of gravity. The light is bent, or curved slightly, nearest the star.

- In a hilly place and in misty weather, light shines past you and casts a giant shadow on mists or clouds. The shadow is surrounded by colored rings. This is called the Brocken Specter.

SPECIAL FX

MANY HANDS MAKE LIGHT WORK

Study shadows like scientists of the past by using candles as a light source. A candle does not cast quite the sharp-edged shadows as a flashlight *(see below)*.

You need

Safety candles and matches, table, white wall, adult supervision.

1. Hold your hand between a lighted candle and the wall. Keep your hand more than 12 inches (30 centimeters) from the candle. Move your hand nearer the wall. Is the shadow bigger or smaller? Is it clearer or more blurred?

2. Put two lighted candles side by side, and hold up your hand again. How many shadows are there? Do they overlap?

3. Carefully move one candle away from the other, and hold up your hand again. Are the shadows farther apart? Trace the light going in straight lines from each candle, past your hand to the wall.

SHARP OR BLURRED?

Light from a point casts a sharper shadow than light from a larger source.

1. Using a flashlight with a narrow beam, shine it to cast a shadow of your hand on the wall.

2. Place tracing paper over the flashlight, and try again. The tracing paper blurs the light source. Is the shadow as clear?

11

MAKING LIGHT

For billions of years, the Sun has made light by **nuclear fusion**. For millions of years, animals have made light by **bioluminescence**. For thousands of years, people have been able to see at night by the light of flames. The light bulb was invented just over one hundred years ago.

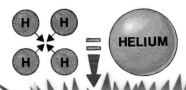

The glowworm is a female beetle that makes a greenish, glowing light. The female does this to attract a male.

*In the Sun, four **atoms** of hydrogen join to produce one atom of helium, giving off energy as light, heat, and in other forms. This is called nuclear fusion.*

Our nearest star, the Sun, is the main source of light for our world. It looks big and bright because it is so close to Earth. But the Sun is actually a fairly small star, a glowing ball of mainly hydrogen gas. It produces huge amounts of light, heat, and other energy by a nuclear fusion reaction. This involves pushing together four atoms of hydrogen with incredible force, so that they join, or fuse.

FAMOUS FIRSTS

LIGHT TO SEE BY

The first evidence of people using fire comes from fossil ashes at Dragon Mountain near Beijing in China. People learned to make flaming torches from long-burning wood. Then they invented wax candles and oil lamps. The candles used slow-burning materials that made a bright yellow flame. In the lamps, oil was soaked into a piece of rope or textile that burned slowly.

This ancient Scottish oil lamp held oil in a seashell.

Over five thousand years ago in Crete and Egypt, the first candles were made using beeswax. Tallow, or solid animal fat — especially from cattle and sheep — became a popular, but smoky, candle fuel.

Caves were fairly safe and sheltered, but dark. Fire produced light and heat for warmth and cooking.

The ancient Egyptians made portable oil lamps from clay and other pottery materials.

Surrounding a flame with a clear glass tube or fixture protected it from going out.

DIY SCIENCE

MAKE YOUR OWN LIGHT

Make your own electric lamp that gives out about the same amount of light as an oil lamp. Could you use this today as your only light source, as in times past?

You need

A small battery (such as an AA), a bulb and socket, brass fasteners, paper clip, plastic bottle, tape, wire.

1. Carefully cut off the top of the bottle. Keep both parts for later use.

2. Wash and dry the parts of the bottle.

3. Screw the bulb into the socket. Then screw a piece of wire to each socket contact, as shown.

4. With tape, attach the end of one wire from the socket to one battery contact.

5. Tape a third length of wire to the other end of the battery. This will go to a switch.

6. Tape the battery securely to the bottle's inside wall. With scissors, cut small holes for the brass fasteners close enough for the paper clip to touch both.

7. Push each wire end out through a hole and attach to a brass fastener. Insert the fasteners in the holes and spread the ends inside. Attach one end of the paper clip to a fastener. Touch the clip to the other fastener to turn on the light.

8. Push the bulb and socket into the neck of the bottle top. Insert the bottle top into the bottle bottom with the bulb facing out.

9. Tape the top to the bottle. Your electric lamp is now ready to use.

The result is one atom of the slightly heavier gas, helium, plus massive amounts of energy.

Nuclear fusion happens constantly in the Sun's interior, using up more than four million tons of hydrogen every second. Luckily, the Sun is so enormous that there is enough hydrogen to last for many millions of years.

Here on Earth, there are many sources of light in nature. A lightning bolt is a huge spark of electrical energy that produces heat, light, and sound. Some animals make light that can be very bright. These include glow-worms and fireflies.

Davy lamp

BRIGHT IDEAS

Long ago, explosive gases seeped through mines so that the flames of lamps often started terrible fires. Humphry Davy (1778-1829) invented a safety lamp by enclosing the flame in a wire mesh to stop its heat from reaching the gases outside. In the nineteenth century, the first electric lamps used a continuous spark called an arc, which flickered noisily and often went out.

In the first electric lamps, an arc sparked between the tips of two carbon rods. But the arc burned away the carbon, so the gap had to be continually adjusted.

In Davy's safety lamp for miners, gases on the outside of the lamp could not get hot enough to explode.

gap

FAMOUS FIRSTS

THE COMING OF THE LIGHT BULB

After the invention of the battery in 1800, many scientists used it to experiment with electricity. But the use of batteries was limited to special equipment in laboratories and factories. All this changed in 1879. English inventor Joseph Swan (1828-1914) and American inventor Thomas Edison (1847-1931) separately produced the first successful light bulbs. The bulbs did not use a flame or spark. A thin **filament** was heated so much by electricity passing through that it glowed white-hot. With this, the age of electricity and inexpensive, powerful light began.

At first, Swan (left) and Edison argued about who invented the light bulb first. But when they realized it would be a long, costly battle, they joined forces. Their factories were soon making millions of bulbs.

Swan's bulb
The very thin filament was mainly carbon.

Edison's bulb
As in Swan's lamp, the glass bulb had most of the air removed. With hardly any oxygen, the filament could not burn up.

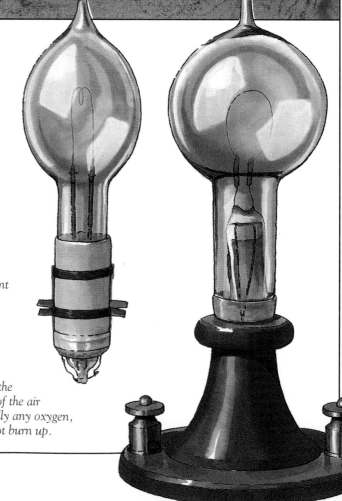

14

MODERN LIGHT BULBS

Compared to the early bulbs of the 1880s, modern bulbs make one hundred times more light for the same electricity. A special gas inside the airtight bulb keeps the filament from burning up for many months.

The filament is a tungsten-based wire, coiled into a tiny corkscrew shape, then coiled again.

ES (Edison screw) base

BC (bayonet cap) base

Retaining pin

The sodium bulb has no filament. It works like an arc lamp, but the yellow glow comes from sodium vapor. Sodium lamps are often used in street lighting.

Electricity goes in and out of the bulb via two metal contacts on the base.

The mirrored spotlight is an incandescent bulb — it has a filament that glows or "incandesces." The bulb's inner silvery coating reflects (see page 24) almost all the light through its clear front.

- In the nineteenth century, city streets were illuminated by gas lamps lighted at dusk and extinguished at dawn.

Even today, remote lighthouses use gas lamps that burn bottled acetylene gas.

Like the sodium bulb, the mercury bulb lacks a filament. The mainly blue glow is made by electricity passing through mercury vapor.

These are not true worms or flies. They are types of beetles. There are many light-making creatures in the sea, including jellyfish, worms, shrimp, and hundreds of types of fish. In most cases of bioluminescence, or "living" light, the glow is made when oxygen from the air combines with a substance called luciferin in the animal's skin. Most methods of making light produce heat as well, such as in flames and lightning. Bioluminescence is unusual because it is "cold" light, with hardly any heat.

There have always been fires in nature, usually started by lightning. But about half a million years ago, our prehistoric ancestors began to control fire for warmth, cooking, defense against wild animals, and light. Many examples have been found of Stone Age campfires, especially in caves. Some have piles of ash several feet (meters) deep, showing that the campfire was used over many years.

A burning flame remained the main source of light for people until about a hundred years ago. Scientists had been working hard to produce light from electricity, either as a continuous spark called an arc or as a thin wire filament that glowed white-hot while electricity passed through it. In 1879, two inventors succeeded with the second method. They were Thomas Edison in America and Joseph Swan in England. Thanks to them, the light bulb was invented. From that time, electric lights have illuminated the world.

Electrical contacts (electrodes)

Fluorescents provide bright light over large areas for use in offices and factories.

THE FLUORESCENT LIGHT
The **fluorescent** light does not have a filament. It works using fluorescence, as described below. French physicist Henri Becquerel made the first simple version of this lamp in 1867. But it did not come into regular use until about 1940 because of problems in manufacturing the tube and getting it to switch on easily.

Physics pioneer Henri Becquerel (1852-1948) was interested in fluorescence and was the first scientist to study radioactivity. He won a Nobel Prize in 1903.

HOW IT WORKS
The fluorescent lamp is a long glass tube containing a mixture of vapors, mainly mercury (which is poisonous). A high voltage of electricity passes from one end of the tube to the other, through the vapor. The electrical energy makes the vapor glow, but with invisible ultraviolet or UV light *(see page 40)*. The special phosphor coating that lines the inside of the tube takes in the energy of the UV light. The phosphor changes this energy into visible light energy, which is seen as a white glow from the tube. The process of taking in the energy of one type of light and changing it into another type or color of light is called fluorescence. Fluorescent light is more efficient and economical than bulbs with filaments.

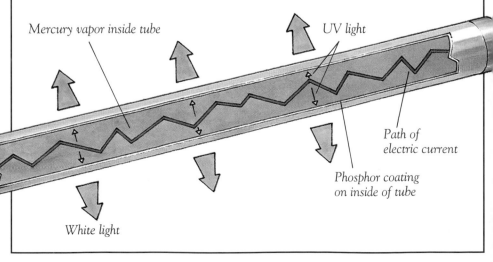

Mercury vapor inside tube

UV light

Path of electric current

Phosphor coating on inside of tube

White light

GLOW IN THE DARK

Some substances take in light energy from bright surroundings, store it for a short time, and release it later. These substances can glow in the dark — a process called **phosphorescence**. Safe phosphorescent substances are used to make certain toys and other items, such as clocks and dog collars, that glow in the dark.

Toy steamroller

Drum

Top

Glow-in-the-dark dominoes

Dolls

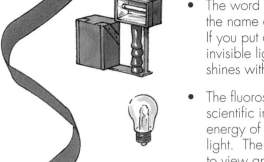

Heat from various sources

- The word *fluorescence* comes from the name of a natural mineral, fluorite. If you put a lump of fluorite under the invisible light from a UV lamp, it shines with an eerie glow.

- The fluoroscope is an important scientific instrument. It converts the energy of invisible X rays into visible light. The fluoroscope can be used to view an X ray of a body and to examine solid substances for flaws.

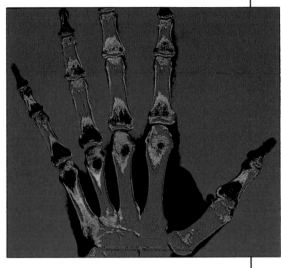

The bones of the hand, revealed by an X ray.

- Light rays cannot pass through humans or animals, but X rays can (in controlled amounts to prevent harm). X rays go through soft parts, such as blood and muscles, easily. But they do not go through hard parts like bones and cartilage. On an X-ray photograph, hard body parts are pale and visible, but soft body parts are dark.

- The metal radium is luminescent — it gives out light. In the 1920s, glow-in-the-dark toys and clock and watch faces used radium-containing paints. But workers got radiation sickness from the radium. The use of radium paint was then stopped.

- Bright colors, like orange and green, are worn by cyclists and others who wish to be highly visible. These are sometimes called luminous or fluorescent colors, but they are actually highly reflective.

DETECTING LIGHT

Humans and animals detect light with the eyes. Humans also have machines, such as cameras and light meters, that record and measure light energy (*see page 22*). Light energy can be converted, or changed, into other forms of energy, such as energy-rich chemicals, heat, or electricity.

Some insects see light that the human eye cannot detect. A bee sees ultraviolet light (see page 40) that reveals patterns on flower petals.

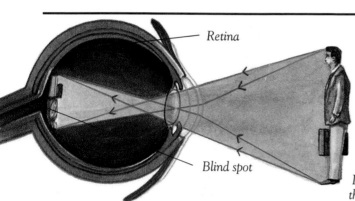

— Retina

— Blind spot

Light shines from objects into the eye and onto the retina. There, chemical changes trigger bursts of electricity that form nerve signals. The signals travel to the brain.

Clams and scallops have tiny jewel-like eyes that do not produce clear vision. They only "see" patches of light or dark.

In order to study and use light, a person must be able to detect it. You are doing this now, using the most familiar of light-detectors — your eyes.

The eyes detect light in a two-stage process. First, light shines into your eyes and onto the **retina**, a very thin layer inside each eyeball. Here, the energy of each tiny patch of light causes chemical changes in substances known as visual pigments.

Second, the chemical changes in the visual pigments trigger tiny bursts of electricity that form nerve signals. These flash along nerves to your brain. This happens at incredible speed. Millions of visual pigments detect millions of tiny patches of light every second in the retina.

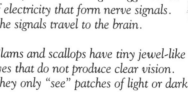

DIY SCIENCE

THROUGH A FLY'S EYES
The fly has eyes with hundreds of separate parts. These are compound eyes. Each one sees a small patch of the scene.

You need
A pencil, cardboard, tracing paper, tape, newspaper.

1. Carefully cut a small hole in cardboard, as shown. Tape the tracing paper over a photo in the newspaper. Put the cardboard over this. Look through the hole at the tiny patch of photo. Is it light or dark?

2. With the pencil, shade the tracing paper through the hole, light or dark as you perceive it. Repeat this one hundred times, moving the hole to different parts of the photo. Lift the tracing paper to see a mosaic-type set of shaded dots — a fly's-eye view.

TRICKS WITH LIGHT

We can make sense of most natural patterns of light detected by our eyes, such as the pattern on the ball *at the top*. But there are also optical illusions that can be puzzling. However, these illusions do not "trick" the eye. The eye simply detects the colors and patterns of light reaching it and passes nerve signals to the brain. Optical illusions trick the *brain* as to how it interprets and makes sense of the signals.

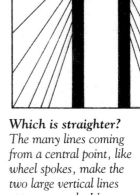

The ball (right) could be covered with raised lumps or small pits. Your brain assumes light comes from above, which it usually does. The shadows cast downward suggest pits, while upward they suggest lumps.

Which is longer? *Guess which straight, central line is longer. Then measure the lengths with a ruler.*

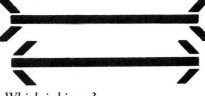

Which is bigger?
The cats in this room look different sizes, with the one on the left being the smallest. But they are all the same size. The effect is due to the lines which make the cats appear to be different distances away.

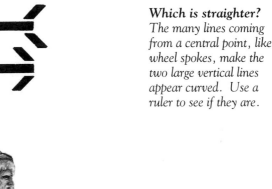

Which is straighter?
The many lines coming from a central point, like wheel spokes, make the two large vertical lines appear curved. Use a ruler to see if they are.

HOW TO FIND YOUR BLIND SPOT

You need
Cardboard, dark crayon.

1. With the crayon, draw two dots on the cardboard, 4 inches (10 cm) apart. Then hold the cardboard about 12 inches (30 cm) from your face. Close one eye. Look at one of the dots with the other eye. Slowly bring the page nearer, still looking at the first dot.

2. When the light rays from the second dot fall on your eye's blind spot, the dot disappears. Now look toward the second dot. The light rays fall on a normal part of your eye's retina. The dot reappears as if by magic!

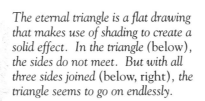

The eternal triangle is a flat drawing that makes use of shading to create a solid effect. In the triangle (below), the sides do not meet. But with all three sides joined (below, right), the triangle seems to go on endlessly.

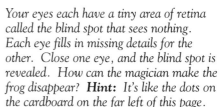

Your eyes each have a tiny area of retina called the blind spot that sees nothing. Each eye fills in missing details for the other. Close one eye, and the blind spot is revealed. How can the magician make the frog disappear? **Hint:** *It's like the dots on the cardboard on the far left of this page.*

19

Incredible numbers of nerve signals flash to the brain. The brain analyzes the flashes, creating a picture of the world with shapes, patterns, and movements in full, living color.

For a time, we can remember what our eyes see, but memories fade. An artist can draw or paint a scene, but this is a personal view that is never completely exact. People in the nineteenth century wanted to invent a device that would detect light accurately and make a permanent record of it.

The result was photography, or "writing with light." The photographic camera uses the same principle as the eye. The energy in light causes changes in a layer of silver-based chemicals called film. This produces a copy, or photograph, of the pattern of light. The first photographs were taken in the 1820s.

Soon, people wanted to record more than single, still photographs. They wanted movement, just as in real life.

FAMOUS FIRSTS

PIONEERS OF PHOTOGRAPHY

In 1727, scientists noticed that certain silver-containing chemicals turned dark when exposed to light. However, it took one hundred years for Joseph Niepce to use this effect to make the first true photograph. Another seventy years passed before photography developed into a practical process, inexpensive and easy enough for almost anyone to use.

Early photographs needed a great deal of light. So the subjects had to sit very still for several minutes.

Joseph Niepce (1765-1833)

William Fox Talbot (1800-1877) invented the negative photograph, with dark areas showing up the lightest. Many positive prints could be made from one negative. He called these calotypes.

Calotype camera

Daguerre cameras had a sliding rear portion. This was moved in or out to focus the picture.

*Like most cameras, Fox Talbot's used a **lens** to focus a clear, sharp picture (see page 32).*

A modern camera fits into a pocket. It can automatically measure light level, focus on a scene, and wind the film.

Video cameras record light not as changed chemicals (like on photographic film), but as tiny patches of magnetism in iron particles that coat the flexible videotape.

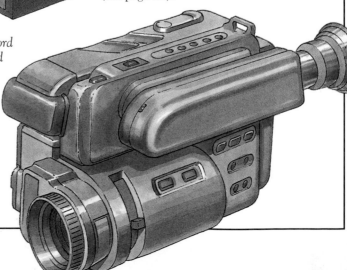

SEE-THROUGH CAMERA
Most cameras have a lens to focus light rays.

You need
Small cardboard box and tube, tracing paper, tape, magnifying glass.

1. Place the tube on one side of the box, and draw a circle around it.

2. Carefully cut out the circle, making a hole. Cut out the entire side of the box that is opposite the hole.

3. Push the tube a little way into the hole, and tape it securely in place.

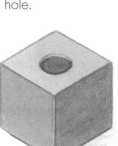

4. Tape tracing paper onto the box in place of the side that was cut out.

5. Hold the magnifying glass (your "lens") over the open end of the tube in the position shown.

6. Point your camera at a well-lighted object. A picture or image of the object forms on the tracing paper. Move the lens back and forth, and watch how the picture becomes clear or blurred. Why is it upside-down?

- Eadweard Muybridge (1830-1904) was a pioneer of fast-action photography, where each picture is taken a very short time after the previous one. In 1877, he photographed a running horse with a bank of twenty-four cameras operated by trip wires. This settled a bet that the horse had all four feet off the ground for a split second — it did. Muybridge also photographed people and other animals in motion.

- Today's fast-action cameras take thousands of pictures each second. They can freeze movements too fast for our eyes to see, such as the rapid beating of an insect's wings.

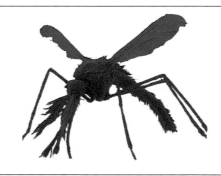

- Color photography lagged behind black-and-white photography. It took a great deal of research to find the right mixture of chemicals, each responding to a different color and brightness of light. It did not become practical until the early 1900s (for stills) and the 1950s (for movies).

Inventors soon devised machines to take, and then show, many still photographs in a fast sequence of about twenty-five photographs per second. The eye cannot distinguish between each of the photos in a fast sequence. The photos blur into each other to create continuous movement. The movie camera and the projection system for displaying the pictures onto a screen were developed in the 1890s.

Then scientists began to work on the idea of not only detecting light, but using its energy to do useful work. However, light's energy is weak when compared to many other forms of energy. The use of light energy had to wait until the development of sensitive electronic circuits during the 1950s and 1960s.

Movie cameras use large rolls of photographic film wound onto two spools in a case above the camera body. The tripod keeps the camera steady so the images are not blurred, yet it lets the camera swing sideways or "pan."

FASCINATING FACTS

THE FIRST MOVIES

During the late 1800s, inventors worked feverishly to make the first movies or motion pictures. The system needed many photographs taken in fast succession. This became possible with celluloid film on a flexible strip, invented in 1887 by American George Eastman. In the 1890s, Thomas Edison's kinetoscope played short movies in a viewbox for one viewer at a time. The movies truly arrived in 1895 with the first film by the Lumière brothers, projected onto a screen for multiple viewers in Paris, France.

Louis Lumière (1864-1948) and his brother Auguste (1862-1954) invented a device called the cinématographe. It was a camera for taking photographs plus a projector that showed them in quick succession on the screen.

The mutascope worked like a flicker-book, showing many photographs in quick succession for one viewer at a time.

Over time, movie cameras became more reliable and portable. They recorded feature films, newsreels, and documentaries.

Inside a movie camera, a strip of film unwinds from one reel, goes past the rear of the lens, and winds onto a take-up spool.

SPECIAL FX

MOVING PICTURES

Zoetropes showed still pictures in quick succession like a movie film.

You need

Cardboard, tape, pencil.

1. Carefully cut a long cardboard strip. Draw about twenty lines to divide it into squares. Draw a figure that moves slightly, from one square or "frame" to the next.

2. Tape the cardboard strip to a cardboard disk, as shown, with the pictures on the outside. Push the pencil through the middle of the disk, and tape it in place.

3. Carefully cut a small hole in another piece of cardboard, and look through this, as shown. On a smooth table, spin your picture wheel fast, like a top. See how the pictures blur into each other to create movement.

FAMOUS FIRSTS

LIGHT POWER

Light is changed into electricity using photoelectric cells, first developed in the 1920s. A photoelectric cell powered by sunlight is called a solar cell. An average cell produces about 0.6-1.0 volts. Cells connected together produce higher voltages. One drawback is that the solar cells only make useful amounts of electricity in very bright light.

Satellites have large fold-out panels covered with solar cells to power their electronic equipment.

The test car Sunraycer, covered with solar cell panels, drove across Australia on power from sunlight.

In highly sunny places, solar cells generate electricity.

Sunlight and artificial light can power watches and calculators that need only tiny amounts of electricity.

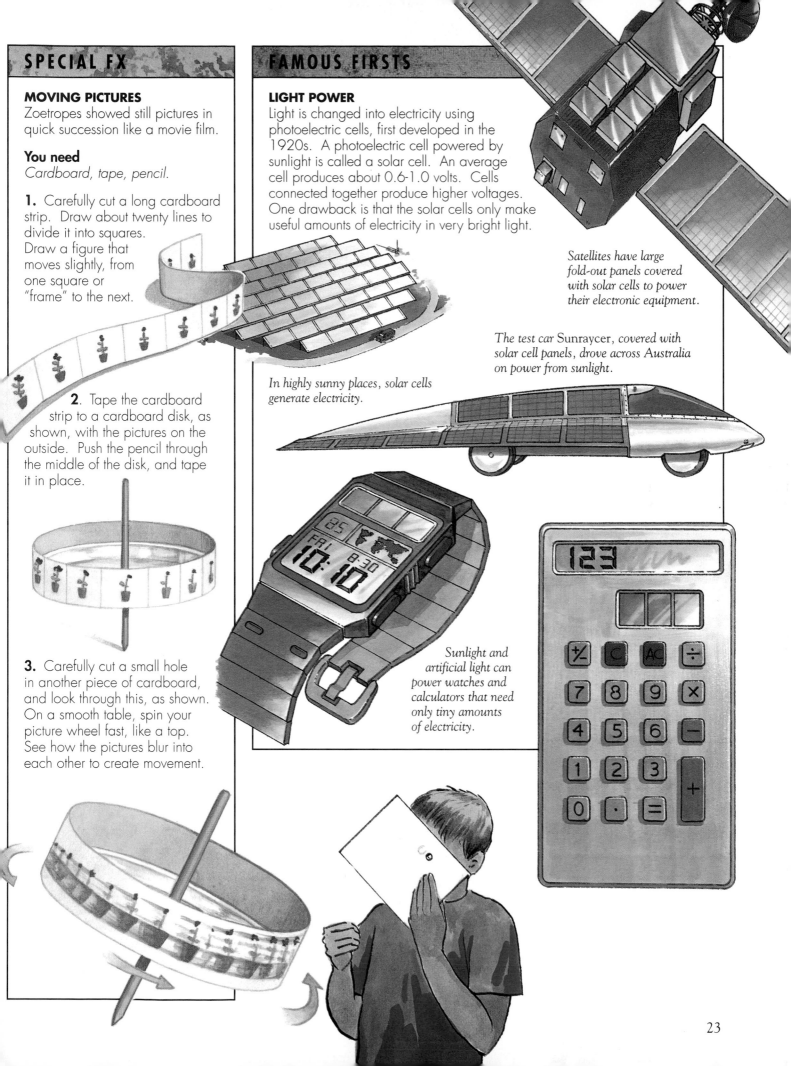

BOUNCING LIGHT

Light from the Sun reflects off your friend and then into your eyes.

Long ago, people looked into a still pool of water and realized they could see their own faces. This happens by the process of light from an object bouncing off a smooth surface and entering our eyes. We call it reflection. There are hundreds of uses for reflection in our world today, from the bathroom mirror to the latest cameras and optic fibers.

Look at a friend on a pond bank. You see light coming to you directly plus light reflecting from the water's surface forming an upside-down image.

Light bounces off most objects. This is how we see them. Light from the Sun or another source bounces from their surfaces and enters our eyes.

However, most surfaces are rough and not shiny. So the light bounces off them in a random way. But a very smooth, shiny surface allows light to bounce off it very precisely, with the same pattern that it had before it arrived at the surface. This arriving light pattern represents a picture or image of whatever it had bounced off before. So a smooth, shiny surface such as a mirror simply passes on, or reflects, the image of the previous object straight into your eyes.

A simple example involves looking in a mirror. Light from the Sun or another source bounces off your face. Some of this light reaches the mirror in a pattern of colors and brightnesses that represents what your face looks like. This light reflects from the mirror's silver-smooth surface in a very precise, accurate way, keeping its pattern. Then it enters your eyes, still carrying the

SPECIAL FX

MIRROR-WRITING
Can you do mirror-writing? This is writing that is back-to-front, so when you see its image in a mirror, it looks normal. The Italian scientist and artist Leonardo da Vinci made many of his notes in mirror-writing.

Leonardo da Vinci (1452-1519)

Can you write like this?

How well can you read backwards without using a mirror?

FAMOUS FIRSTS

A TREASURED BOOK
The Egyptian physicist Alhazen (965-1038) studied flat and curved mirrors, as well as lenses and the eye. His book *The Treasury of Optics* presented ideas about colors and pinhole cameras. Alhazen was one of the first scientists to develop the law of reflection, shown *opposite*.

Unlike many of his fellow scientists, Alhazen believed that light went from objects into the eye, rather than coming out of the eye onto objects. Alhazen also studied irrigation ideas for the Nile River and pretended he was insane for many years to avoid his king's displeasure.

THE LAW OF REFLECTION

You need
A flashlight, sheets of cardboard, a mirror, a protractor, a pencil, a dark place.

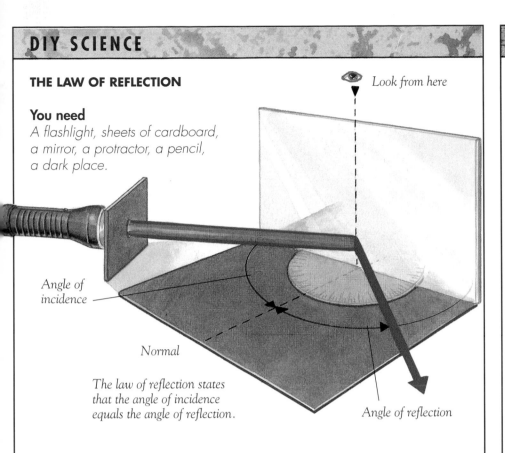

Look from here

Angle of incidence

Normal

The law of reflection states that the angle of incidence equals the angle of reflection.

Angle of reflection

1. Cut a hole in a sheet of cardboard. Tape the cardboard over a flashlight's lens. Arrange the flashlight, a mirror, and another sheet of cardboard, as pictured. Place a protractor at the point where the flashlight reflects off the mirror.

2. Draw a line at 90° to the mirror, called the "normal." For different flashlight positions, measure the angle between the flashlight beam and the normal, and the reflected beam and the normal. They should be equal.

FASCINATING FACTS

A shaving mirror gives an enlarged, or magnified, view.

The first mirrors were simply bowls of water. Later, polished metals, such as bronze, were used as mirrors by the ancient Egyptians.

CURVED MIRRORS

The shiny surface of a spoon acts as a curved mirror. Look at each side to see how the images differ. On the inner or **concave** side, you may see a tiny upside-down image of your face. On the bulging or **convex** side, you see a wide-angle, upright view called a virtual image.

Concave mirror

Convex mirror

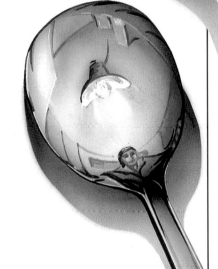

Concave mirror
The light rays come together in front of the spoon at a point called the focus. There they cross over and spread out.

Convex mirror
The light rays reflect outward and appear to come from behind the spoon.

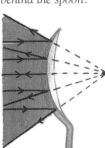

pattern of colors and brightnesses that it had when it left your face. So you see a picture of your own face — a reflection, or mirror-image.

Many scientists of ancient times thought light was produced in the eye. They thought it came out of the eyes and shone onto the surroundings, creating pictures of objects in the same way a movie projector shines pictures of objects onto a screen. In the eleventh century, the Egyptian scientist Alhazen (*see page 24*) thought light moved in the opposite direction — from objects into the eye. His work laid part of the foundation for **optics** — the science and study of light.

The ancient Greeks and Romans had some understanding of the basic science of reflection. They used dark-colored bowls of water for mirrors. They also made mirrors from flat sheets of highly polished metal, such as bronze. When glass and silvered mirrors became available in the fourteenth century, people could see clearer, sharper images in their "looking glasses."

Gradually, more effective mirrors found their way into everyday life. Optical devices, such as the **periscope**, were invented. The periscope uses reflections from two mirrors to see over the top of or around the side of an object. It was first commonly used in the trench warfare of the nineteenth century. In the optical toy called the **kaleidoscope**, the reflection of objects in one mirror is itself reflected in another mirror. The kaleidoscope was invented by

(see page 24)

SPECIAL FX

THE COLORFUL KALEIDOSCOPE

You need
Sheets of cardboard, scissors, tracing paper, pencil, tape, two small plastic-edged mirrors, colored beads, flashlight.

1. Fold and tape a sheet of cardboard into a triangular tube, as shown.

2. Place the triangular tube upright on another sheet of cardboard, and draw around it. Cut the shape out.

3. Carefully cut a small viewing hole in this piece, about 1 inch (3 cm) across.

4. Tape the mirrors inside the tube, on two sides. Then tape the cardboard end into place.

5. Follow step 2 but use tracing paper and do not cut a viewing hole in it. Tape the tracing paper on the other end.

6. Place some colored beads into your kaleidoscope onto the tracing paper bottom. Shine a flashlight from below.

FASCINATING FACTS

GHOSTLY ILLUSION
The "Pepper's ghost" is a large, upright glass sheet on a theater stage. The glass works as both window and mirror. The audience can see objects behind it and also reflections of objects located at the side of the stage. With careful lighting, a person at the side of the stage looks like a "ghost" and seems to walk through objects.

SEEING AROUND CORNERS

You need
Milk carton, pencil, scissors, cardboard, two small plastic-edged mirrors, adult supervision.

1. Using a triangle of cardboard, draw a line on the top part of one side of the milk carton, as shown. Draw a line sloping the same way on the lower part of the carton.

2. Carefully cut a slit along the lines, which should be just large enough to push the mirrors through.

3. Draw and cut slits on the opposite side of the box.

Upper mirror has reflecting side down

4. Push a mirror through each pair of slits, as shown. Adjust the slits as necessary for a good fit.

Lower mirror has reflecting side up

5. Carefully cut a viewing hole in front of the upper mirror, so you can see its reflecting side. Cut another viewing window behind the lower mirror, again so you can see its reflective surface.

6. Look into your periscope, as shown. You see an object reflected in the first mirror, then in the second one. Is the view you see a back-to-front mirror image, or the right way around?

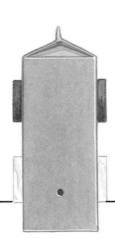

- Rigid periscope-type devices called endoscopes were once used to look into the body to check for illness and disease. Modern, flexible versions use fiber optics *(see page 45)*.

- Complicated and delicate periscopes over 30 feet (10 meters) long are used on submarines. Only the top of the periscope sticks out of the water, while the submarine stays out of sight below.

A submarine periscope shows the view at the surface.

Scottish physicist David Brewster (1781-1868), who specialized in the reflection and polarization of light (*see page 29*). Brewster also improved the design of lighthouses.

Some substances do not reflect light — they let light pass through. If some of the light gets through but is scattered, and you can see the light and vague shapes on the other side, the substance is **translucent**. If light passes through without scattering and shapes are clearly seen, the substance is **transparent**.

One of the most useful transparent substances is glass, which was invented in ancient Egypt. Glass came into common use during Roman times for bowls, goblets, and other containers, and for decorative beads and ornaments. Glass for windows was not needed in countries where the climate was mild. Glass windows became common in northern Europe during medieval times. They kept the wind and rain out but let light in. A house with glass windows was a sign of wealth.

Colored glass is made by adding certain substances during the glass-making process. Chromium is used to make green glass, copper or selenium for red, and cobalt or copper for blue. Pieces of colored glass are used to make the impressive stained-glass windows in churches. Today, transparent plastics such as acrylic have taken over some of glass's uses. Plastics are much lighter than glass and do not shatter. But plastics are also softer and, therefore, scratch more easily.

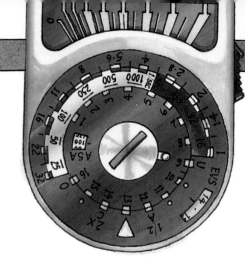

DIY SCIENCE

WHICH FLASHLIGHT IS BRIGHTEST?

You need
Selection of flashlights, tracing paper.

1. This simple light meter checks which flashlight is brightest. In the same dim conditions for each flashlight, put sheets of tracing paper over each flashlight until you can no longer see the light shining through. The flashlight that needs the most sheets is brightest.

Light meters use sensitive electronic circuits to measure the amount of light energy changing to electrical energy.

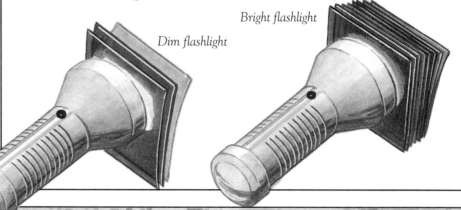

Bright flashlight

Dim flashlight

SPECIAL FX

LIGHT UP A SCENE

You need
Scissors, cardboard, tape, different colored sheets of transparent plastic or cellophane.

1. Make a stained-glass window like those in churches. Draw a scene on cardboard first.

2. Carefully cut various pieces from the colored sheets to fit the scene. Tape them together over the cardboard. Then cut the inside of the cardboard away, leaving a frame for your stained-glass window scene.

Hold a flashlight behind the window to make the colors brighter.

REFLECTING TWISTED LIGHT: THE LCD

Think of light as waves **undulating** in all directions. When all the waves undulate in the same direction, this is known as **polarized** light. An LCD (Liquid Crystal Display), such as the display on a calculator, does not give out light. It uses polarization and reflection.

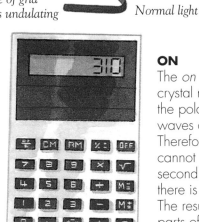

Polarized light

Screen

Normal light

A polarizing screen is a type of grid that lets through only waves undulating in a certain direction.

OFF
The front screen polarizes the light waves. The *off* crystal twists them. The waves go through a second screen, reflect from the back, and follow the reverse path out. The reflection makes the area look light.

ON
The *on* parts of the crystal no longer twist the polarized light waves at right angles. Therefore, they cannot go through the second screen, and there is no reflection. The result is these parts of the crystal look dark.

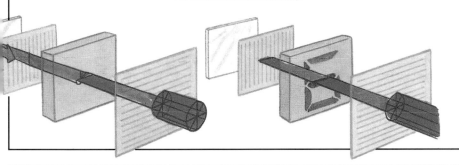

- When light reflects from certain surfaces, such as water, it is partly polarized. Polarized sunglasses *(right)* help filter out unwanted light waves and reduce glare from reflections.

- Polarized sunglasses help pilots, drivers, skiers, sailors, and other people who may be troubled by shiny surfaces, reflections, and glare.

- Bees detect light that humans cannot, such as ultraviolet light *(see page 40)*. They can also see the direction of polarization in light. Clouds polarize light from the Sun. So even on cloudy days, bees know the position of the Sun from its polarized light.

SHADES TO BLACK

You need
Two pairs of Polaroid (polarizing) sunglasses.

1. Hold the two pairs of sunglasses at the same angle so that one lens is behind the other, as shown. Look through, and note the darkness of the view.

2. Turn one pair, keeping the other steady. The view slowly darkens. The rear pair polarizes the light waves. As the other pair twists to right angles, none of the waves can get through its lens.

No light gets through Polaroid lenses at right angles.

BENDING LIGHT

I f you see a coin on the bottom of a swimming pool, and you want to reach down and get it, beware! At a quick glance, the pool may seem shallow. But light bends when it goes from one substance, such as water, to another, such as air. A pool of water is always deeper than it looks.

Light refracts as it passes from water to air. The fish looks nearer the surface than it actually is.

Light refracted

Apparent position of fish

Real position of fish

The bending of light when it goes from one substance to another is called refraction. Light bends because the speed of light changes as it passes across the boundary between different substances. This happens, for example, when light goes from air into glass or water — and when it comes back out into the air.

Refraction involves two angles (*see illustration at right*). The angle between the incident (or striking) ray and the normal is called the angle of incidence. The angle between the refracted ray and the normal is called the angle of refraction. "Normal" is a line at **right angles** to the surface.

Ancient people probably knew about refraction. Perhaps they fished by standing on the bank and hurling a spear into the water. However, they would have soon realized that, even though their aim seemed accurate, the spear always missed the fish. Aiming the spear below the fish is more successful. This is because the light from the fish refracts, or bends, toward the horizontal as it

FAMOUS FIRSTS

Angle of incidence

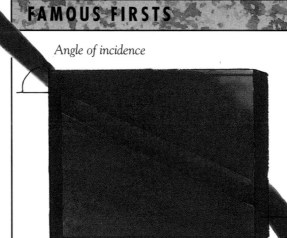

Willebrord Snell (1580-1626) was a Dutch physicist and mapmaker. He was professor of mathematics at Leiden University.

Angle of refraction

In this view of a straw in a glass of water, there is only one straw. But refraction of light by the glass and water makes it appear as if there are two.

HOW MUCH BENDING?
Ancient Egyptians such as Alhazen *(see page 24)* studied refraction but could not predict it precisely. The scientific law describing the exact amount of refraction that occurs was discovered in 1621 by Willebrord Snell. The angles of the light before refraction have a mathematical relationship, depending on the substances concerned. These angles are measured between the beam of light and the "normal" (a line at right angles to the surface). The refracting power of a substance — how much it bends light — is called its refractive index.

THE POWER OF REFRACTION

You can recreate some of Snell's experiments on refraction using everyday items. To compare the refracting power of various liquids, you will need a transparent tray, perhaps from a frozen food item. It must have upright sides, not sloping sides.

You need

Flashlight, cardboard with a slit, large sheet of paper, pencil, protractor, transparent tray, transparent liquids (such as water and cooking oil).

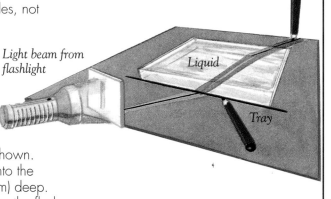

Light beam from flashlight

Liquid

Tray

1. Arrange the flashlight, slit cardboard, food tray, and large paper sheet as shown. Put the first test liquid into the tray, 2-3 inches (5-7 cm) deep. In dark conditions, shine the flashlight through the slit at the tray.

2. With the protractor, measure the angles of incidence and refraction, as shown in the diagram on the right. Try another test liquid, with the flashlight at the same angle of incidence. Is the angle of refraction the same?

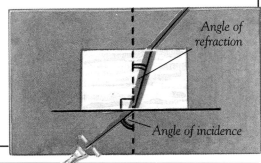

Normal

Angle of refraction

Angle of incidence

FASCINATING FACTS

- Sometimes light is refracted as it passes from air at a certain temperature into warmer or cooler air. This is the basis of a mirage. With a mirage, you see an image of an object that is not really there.

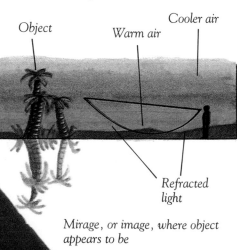

Object

Warm air

Cooler air

Refracted light

Mirage, or image, where object appears to be

Mirages can occur at sea. In the illustration and photograph below, the real island is at the top. Its reflection on the boundary between warm and cool air, just above the sea's surface, is at the bottom.

When light arrives at a boundary between air and water, it may not be refracted into the water. It may be reflected back into the air, as if from a mirror. The angle of incidence must be great for this to happen. It is called total internal reflection and is the basis of fiber optics *(see page 45).*

REFRACTION TO REFLECTION

You need

Flashlight, clear tank of water, white cardboard.

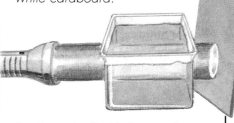

1. Shine the flashlight at right angles to the side of the tank. The angle of incidence is zero. The beam passes straight through, with no refraction.

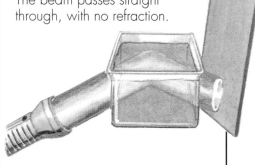

2. Tilt the flashlight up so the beam shines up into the water. It should arrive at the under-surface at a shallow angle (a large angle of incidence).

3. The beam should reflect from the under-surface, like a mirror, rather than pass through into the air.

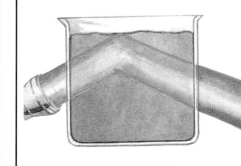

leaves the water and travels to the eyes. The brain guesses that the light is traveling in straight lines. So it follows the line of sight into the water and sees an image of the fish in a certain place. But the real position of the fish is slightly lower.

Refraction can also happen between layers of air of different temperatures. This is the basis of the mysterious image called the **mirage** (see page 31) that is often seen in deserts or above hot, dark blacktop roads.

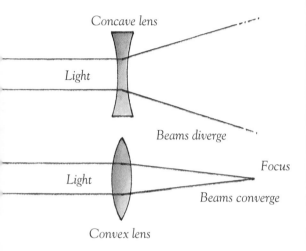

Concave lens

Light

Beams diverge

Light

Focus

Beams converge

Convex lens

There are two basic lens shapes. A concave lens is curved inward and makes light beams spread out, or diverge. A convex lens is bulging and makes light beams come together, or converge, to a point called the focus. The lenses in eyeglasses correct sight problems caused by the eye's own lens or the size of the eyeball. In nearsightedness, for example, the eye's lens is too strong, or the eyeball is too big, and the images come to a focus in front of the retina.

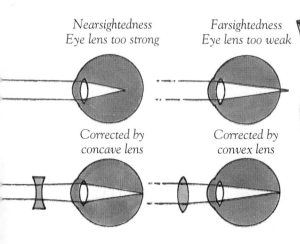

*Nearsightedness
Eye lens too strong*

*Farsightedness
Eye lens too weak*

*Corrected by
concave lens*

*Corrected by
convex lens*

SPECIAL FACTS

SEEING STARS
A shaving mirror has a gentle bulge or outward curve like a convex lens. This produces the effect of magnifying the image you see, just like the underside of a spoon does *(see page 25)*. You can use this type of magnification to get a closer look at the Moon and stars.

You need
Shaving mirror, magnifying glass, flat mirror.

1. On a moonlit night, place the shaving mirror near a window so it reflects the Moon into the flat mirror, as shown. Look at the reflection in the flat mirror through the magnifying glass.

2. The shaving mirror is curved so that it magnifies the image. This enlarged image is made even bigger by the magnifying glass. **Warning:** Never do this during the day. Looking at the Sun can harm your eyes.

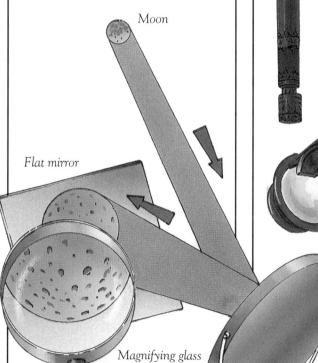

Moon

Flat mirror

Magnifying glass

Shaving mirror

FAMOUS FIRSTS

SEEING INTO OUTER SPACE
The telescope, invented in Holland in 1608, has two or more lenses and makes faraway objects appear much closer than they are. Galileo used telescopes to study our own Moon and the nearby planets and their moons.

Galileo Galilei (1564-1642) used telescopes from about 1609. In his book, Sidereal Messenger (1610), he described mountains on Earth's Moon and moons around the planet Jupiter.

This is a replica of one of Galileo's early telescopes. It magnified objects by about thirty times.

Secondary lense

Eyepiece lens

REFRACTING TELESCOPE

In a refracting telescope, light rays from an object pass through a convex lens, are bent or refracted to a focal point, and form an image. The principle is shown in the diagram below.

A refracting telescope is a closed tube. At the viewing end is an eyepiece lens. At the other end is the objective lens that refracts light from the object being viewed.

Objective lens

REFLECTING TELESCOPE

In a reflecting telescope, light rays from an object are reflected by a concave mirror to a focal point and form an image *(see diagram below).*

Sir Isaac Newton designed the first reflecting telescope in the 1660s.

The observer looks into a reflecting telescope at a small, secondary mirror. The advantage of mirrors over lenses is that they do not split light into its colors as much as lenses do (see page 36) for a clearer, sharper image.

FASCINATING FACTS

- The largest refracting telescope in the world is at Yerkes Observatory in Williams Bay, Wisconsin. Its main lens is almost 40 inches (101 cm) across.

- The largest reflecting telescope is at the Keck Observatory on Mauna Kea in Hawaii. Its main mirror is almost 33 feet (10 m) across and is made of thirty-six separate segments.

The largest single-mirror reflecting telescope (below) is at Mount Palomar, California. The mirror is 200 inches (508 cm) across.

You can see a simple example of refraction by putting a pencil into a glass of water. The lower part of the pencil looks bent at an angle, compared to the upper part. The bend is at the place where the pencil meets the surface of the water. Of course, common sense tells us that the pencil is not really bent. It is an optical illusion — a trick of the light that fools the eyes and brain (*see page 30*). This particular illusion is so common that we get used to it and do not notice it as anything remarkable.

Refraction is put to use in all types of equipment and devices in the form of lenses. A lens is a transparent substance, such as glass or plastic, that has a curved shape. Light is refracted in a certain way as it passes through a lens, depending on the shape of the lens. Opticians are constantly trying to produce new, clear glass and plastics with higher indexes of refraction than before. This enables them to make eyeglasses and contact lenses that are thinner and lighter.

Lenses correct eyesight problems caused by the incorrect shape of the eye's own lens. They make things seem nearer in telescopes, and make things look bigger in microscopes. Many advances in the understanding of refraction and lenses occurred in the 1600s with the invention of the telescope and microscope, and the discovery of the law of refraction by Willebrord Snell (*see page 30*).

FAMOUS FIRSTS

SEEING INTO INNER SPACE

A microscope, like a telescope, makes things appear larger. It has one or more lenses. The curvature of the lenses and the distance between them is adjusted to look at very tiny objects, rather than at very distant ones as in the telescope. The microscope was invented in the 1590s by Dutch craftsman Zacharias Janssen.

Dutch naturalist Antonie van Leeuwenhoek (1632-1723) made single-lens microscopes.

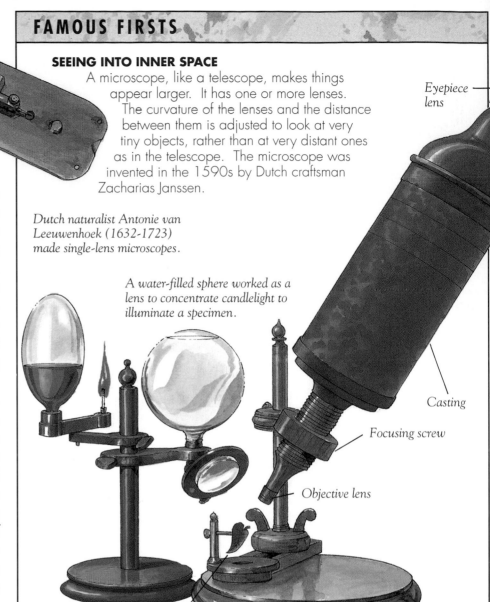

A water-filled sphere worked as a lens to concentrate candlelight to illuminate a specimen.

Eyepiece lens

Casting

Focusing screw

Objective lens

Specimen

DIY SCIENCE

MAKE A MICROSCOPE

You need
Drinking glass, aluminum foil, scissors, tape, modeling clay, small mirror, water.

1. Fold the foil as shown to make a thick strip. With scissors, put a small hole in its center.

2. As shown, bend the strip, and tape it to the glass. Place a mirror over a ball of clay. Place the glass on top.

3. Put a small drop of water in the hole of the foil for a lens. Put a specimen, such as a mosquito, directly underneath the hole for viewing.

Specimen

Mirror reflects light to illuminate specimen

DIY SCIENCE

Long ago, people used water-filled bowls as magnifying lenses for detailed tasks such as sewing and lace-making. This device became known as a lacemaker's condenser.

MAKE A MAGNIFYING GLASS

You need
A clear glass or plastic jar with lid, water.

Fill a jar with water, and put its lid back on. Place the jar over a newspaper or magazine article. See how it acts like a lens to magnify the print.

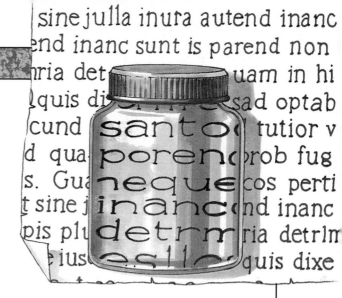

SPECIAL FX

MAKE GIANT SHADOWS!

You need *Flashlight, object such as a fork, eyeglass lens with concave shape for near-sightedness.*

Shine the flashlight on a wall about 3 feet (1 m) away. Position the fork so it casts its shadow on the wall. Put the concave lens in between the fork and flashlight. The lens makes the beam spread out, enlarging the shadow.

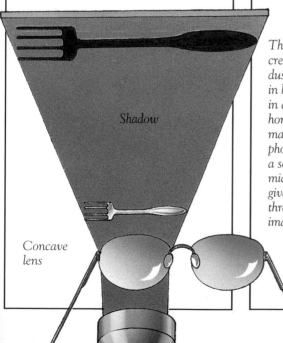

Concave lens

FASCINATING FACTS

- There are several types of microscopes. Those using light can magnify up to 1,000 or 2,000 times. Any bigger, and the view becomes blurred.

- An electron microscope does not use light. It uses beams of atomic particles called electrons. These are focused by magnetic lenses. An electron microscope can magnify objects much more than a microscope using light — in some cases, over one million times. This allows the shapes of individual large molecules to be seen.

The electron microscope is a large and expensive device. The electrons are detected and displayed as a visual image on a television screen.

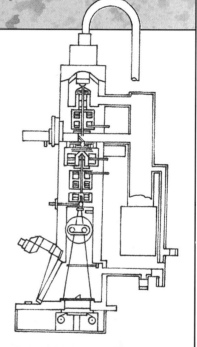

This is a tiny creature called the dust mite. It lives in household dust in even the cleanest homes. It has been magnified and photographed using a scanning electron microscope, which gives a realistic three-dimensional image.

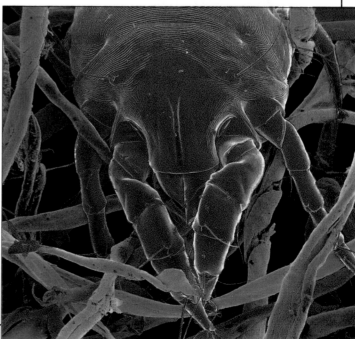

COLORED LIGHT

White light

Glass of water acts as prism

White light split into colors

Look around at the colors of objects. See how they vary from reds and oranges to yellows, greens, blues, and violets — all the colors of the rainbow. They can be bright or dull, vivid or pale. Colors give great pleasure, from beautiful works of art to flowers and birds. Colors also provide information, such as the red, green, and yellow colors of a stoplight.

Raindrops refract sunlight, splitting it into the colors of the spectrum.

So far in this book, we have seen light being made and detected and bouncing and bending. We have referred to white light and called it "light" as though it is a single thing. But it is not. White light is a mixture of colors — all the colors of the rainbow. This extraordinary fact was demonstrated by one of the greatest scientists of all time, Sir Isaac Newton, in about 1665.

In Newton's time, most scientists believed that white light was a single, pure substance. This idea dated back to the time of Aristotle in ancient Greece. People observed that raindrops seemed to turn white light into colors. But they thought that the water droplets added the colors.

FAMOUS FIRSTS

NEWTON AND THE PRISM

In 1665, Sir Isaac Newton began doing experiments with light. In his day, glass **prisms** were available from traveling fairs as curiosities. Newton used the triangle-shaped blocks of glass with angled sides in his experiments. He observed a narrow beam of white sunlight as it passed through the prism. At a certain angle, the beam that emerged was wider, and it looked like a miniature rainbow — the **spectrum**.

Newton suggested that the different colors that made up white light split up because the prism refracted them by different amounts. This was the opposite view from that of most other scientists. They believed that colors were made by adding something to white light.

Sir Isaac Newton (1642-1727) made tremendous advances in many areas of science, especially in describing the force of gravity and how things move.

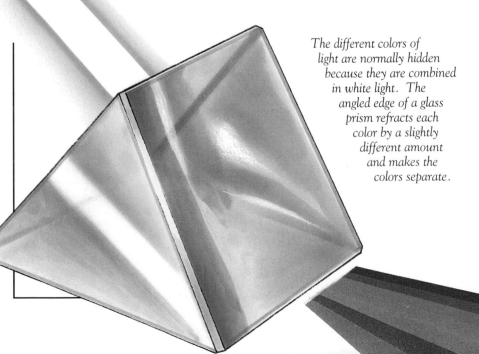

The different colors of light are normally hidden because they are combined in white light. The angled edge of a glass prism refracts each color by a slightly different amount and makes the colors separate.

36

WHITE INTO COLORS

You can repeat two of Newton's famous experiments. The first shows that white light can be split into colors, but that each color cannot be split any farther. The second shows that the various colors obtained by splitting white light can be combined back into white light again. You may be able to obtain a prism from a science supply store or a camera store.

You need

Powerful flashlight with narrow white beam, two prisms, cardboard.

1. In a darkened place, shine the flashlight on a prism. Move the flashlight so the beam reaches the prism's surface at the appropriate angle to produce the colors of the spectrum.

2. Shine one color through a slit in the cardboard and through the second prism. The beam may spread wider, but is it split into any more colors?

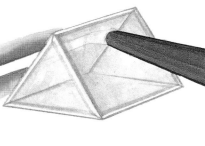

3. For the second experiment, arrange the flashlight and prism to produce a spectrum, as in step 1.

4. Position the second prism as shown so it recombines the colors. The result is white light again.

PRIMARY COLORS

To make white light, you do not need all the colors of the spectrum. Three are enough — red, green, and blue. They are called the primary colors of light, and they combine to make white light. Pigments work in a similar way but give the opposite result. The three primary colors of pigments are yellow, cyan, and magenta, and they combine to make black.

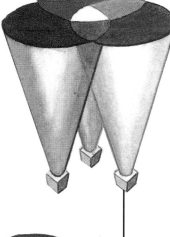

The three primary colors of light from three tinted flashlight beams combine to make white light.

The three primary colors of pigments take away all light, so none is reflected. This results in the color black.

CHANGING COLORS

• The color of an object depends partly on the angle at which light reflects from it. As the Sun moves across the sky, the angle of its rays change, and so do the precise colors and hues of objects.

Uluru (Ayer's Rock) in Australia at dawn.

Uluru at dusk.

Newton showed that white light was really a mixture or combination of the light of different colors. We call the colors the spectrum, or colors of the rainbow. They are commonly thought of as the following seven colors — red, orange, yellow, green, blue, indigo, and violet. But if you look carefully at a real spectrum or the pictures in this book, you see that the colors are not separate and distinct. They change gradually. One merges into the next. The spectrum is continuous, rather than made of sharp steps of distinct colors.

After Newton's discovery, scientists continued to study color, both in light and in the coloring substances called pigments. Paints contain concentrated pigments that change the color of whatever they are spread upon. Gradually, scientists discovered the relationship between color, light, and pigments. This explains why roses are red, and violets are blue — as follows:

Only certain objects, like the Sun or a light bulb, give out light. Most of these light sources make a white or yellowish light because they contain a combination of all the other colors.

We are able to see the other objects in our world because they reflect light. Each object is a certain color because of the color of the light it reflects. In turn, this depends on the types of pigments the object contains.

Pigments do not make or create colors. Only objects that emit light, such as a pocket flashlight or the Sun, create colored light. Pigments take in or absorb colors. For example, imagine white light shining on a tomato. The white light contains all the colors of the spectrum. The pigments in

THE DYE INDUSTRY

For centuries, people used paints and dyes made from the natural pigments in flowers, minerals, and animals. In 1856, William Perkin tried to make medicine from a natural tar. But instead, he developed a shining, mauve-purple substance. It was one of the first artificial dyes. Today, dyes are part of a vital industry that produces colored textiles and materials resulting in everything from T-shirts to carpeting.

English chemist William Perkin (1838-1907)

Yellow dye is made from the extract of certain plants, such as broom.

Ultramarine blue comes from a natural precious stone called lapis lazuli.

Black comes from the soot or carbon left by burning oils, such as linseed oil.

Red comes from the chemical cinnabar or from plants such as basil or beets.

DIY SCIENCE

SEPARATING PIGMENTS

The various inks in pens, especially the dark colors, are usually made by combining several different pigments. The colors can be separated by a process called chromatography.

You need

Tray of water, strips of newspaper, string, paper clips, colored pens with water-soluble inks.

Draw a different colored spot at the base of each strip of newspaper. Hang the strips, as shown, with their bases dipping in the water. The water soaks upward onto each strip, carrying particles of each pigment. The pigments separate according to particle size.

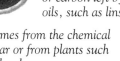

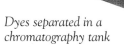

Dyes separated in a chromatography tank

COLORS BACK TO WHITE

The color wheel was devised by Sir Isaac Newton to do the reverse of his famous light-splitting experiment. The idea is to join the colors of the rainbow to produce white light.

You need

Cardboard, scissors, colored pens or paints, pencil.

1. Cut a 4-inch (10-cm) disk from cardboard. Divide it into equal segments. Color the segments like the spectrum, with one set in each half.

2. Push a pencil through the cardboard disk's center. Spin it fast, like a top. The colors merge back together to make white, or at least a light gray or brown.

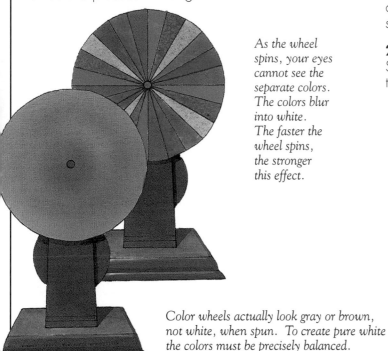

As the wheel spins, your eyes cannot see the separate colors. The colors blur into white. The faster the wheel spins, the stronger this effect.

Color wheels actually look gray or brown, not white, when spun. To create pure white the colors must be precisely balanced.

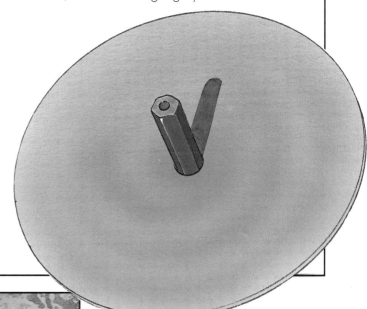

SPECIAL FX

SEEING INVISIBLE COLORS

When your eyes look at strong colors for a period of time, the cells in the sensitive retina of the eye that respond to the colors become "tired." If you then look away, you may see ghost colors which are opposite, or complementary, to the original colors. This is a harmless after-effect. Stare hard at one of the colored patterns here for twenty seconds. Then quickly look away at a plain white area. Can you see ghost colors for a few seconds? Draw a chart of each color's complementary one.

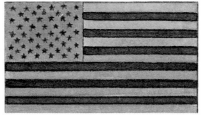

FASCINATING FACTS

- In many countries around the world, green is the color for "go." Red is the color that represents "stop" or a warning or danger. Why is this? Could it be that blood is red?

Red is the symbol for "stop" on traffic lights throughout the world.

the skin of the tomato absorb most of these colors so that, in effect, they disappear. However, the tomato skin's pigments do not absorb the light in the red part of the spectrum. They reflect it. So the only light reflecting off the tomato is the red part of the spectrum. This is the light that reaches your eyes, and you see the tomato as red.

The same happens when light falls on a leaf. But in this case, the color reflected is green from the middle of the spectrum. However, the light at the red and blue ends of the spectrum is absorbed by the leaf, and its energy is trapped by the process of photosynthesis (see page 9). If only green light were directed on a plant, it would still appear green, but it would soon die. The green chemical in plants that takes in light energy is called chlorophyll. However, some plants, such as seaweed, are not green. They are brown or red. This is because they contain different chemicals for photosynthesis, known as xanthophyll or carotene.

A BIGGER SPECTRUM
In 1865, James Clerk Maxwell showed that light was one part of a huge range of energy that has the same basic form. This electromagnetic spectrum is made of waves or rays. One wavelength is the distance from a point on one wave, such as the crest or peak, to the same point on the next wave.

Superhigh radio waves have wavelengths of about 2/3 mile (1 km).

Television radio waves are only a few feet (meters) long.

Radar radio waves are about 4 inches (10 cm) long.

Microwaves have wavelengths of less than .5 inch (1 cm).

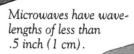

Infrared waves have wavelengths slightly longer than those of red light.

Visible light waves are the only electromagnetic waves the eye detects. The other waves are all around, but we cannot see them.

Ultraviolet waves are shorter than violet light.

James Clerk Maxwell (1831-1879) used mathematics to make his discoveries.

X rays have very short wavelengths. Ten million of them stretch to only .0394 inch (1 millimeter).

Gamma and cosmic rays are incredibly short waves from space and nuclear reactions. These can be dangerous to living things.

FASCINATING FACTS

- Certain insects, such as bees, can see ultraviolet rays at one end of the visible spectrum. Other animals can see infrared rays at the other end. Pit viper snakes have organs under their eyes that sense the infrared rays coming from their warm-blooded prey.

THE COLOR BOX

You can study the way light and pigments work by using a flashlight that has filters to eliminate certain colors of light and by examining colored objects whose surfaces only reflect certain colors of light.

You need

Flashlight, colored transparent plastic filters, pieces of fruit, a box such as a shoe box, scissors, tape.

1. Cut a window in one end of the box to shine the flashlight through, and a hole in the top to look through. Do the experiments in darkened surroundings. Place a red filter in the window. Put red, yellow, and green apples in the box.

2. Shine the flashlight in. The red filter removes all colors from the white beam, except red. The red apple reflects this and looks red. The yellow apple reflects some red light and looks a duller red. But the green apple has no green light to reflect, and it cannot reflect any other colors. So it appears black.

3. Try other colored fruits and filters, and see if you can predict the results.

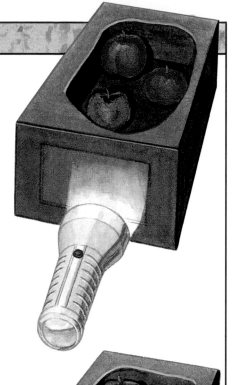

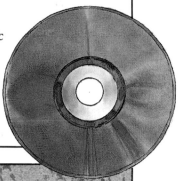

A soap-and-water film on this light bulb produces what are known as interference fringes.

A thin, transparent film of soap or oil over an object causes light to be reflected from two surfaces. The surfaces are so close together that the waves interfere with each other and produce beautiful rainbow patterns called interference patterns.

The microscopic pits on a compact disc reflect light in a rainbow of interference colors.

FAMOUS FIRSTS

WHEN LIGHT INTERFERES

English scientist Thomas Young (1773-1829) experimented with interference patterns. The patterns can be explained only if light is in the form of waves, not particles. Light will pass through small slits close together, and the beams on the other side will spread out and overlap as they reach a screen. If the waves hit the screen in step or in phase, peak to peak, they will make a bright patch. If one wave is a peak and the other is a trough, they cancel each other out, and a dark patch results.

Waves

Particles

If light were in particles, the particles would pass through the slits without making interference patterns (left).

Bright

Dark

When light waves pass through two narrow, close slits, they create dark and bright stripes, colored fringes, and other interference patterns (right).

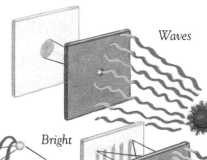

MAKING LIGHT WORK

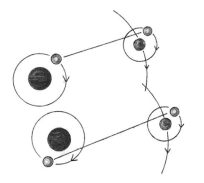

In our modern world, light is put to work in an amazing variety of ways. Sunlight is trapped and turned into electricity and other forms of energy more and more effectively as time goes by. And we are using a special form of light, the laser, in many ways — from eye surgery to cutting industrial metals to reading sounds and images from compact discs.

In the seventeenth century, most scientists believed that light had infinite speed — it took no time at all for light to travel from one place to another. Further experiments showed that the speed of light is finite, although it is still incredibly fast. Light travels 186,420 miles (300,000 km) in one second through space. It travels slower in substances such as glass and water.

It was also believed that light passing through the same substance always traveled in straight lines. But physicist Albert Einstein showed that light can travel in a curve under the pull of a star's gravity.

FAMOUS FIRSTS

CURVED LIGHT
Albert Einstein (1879-1955) used mathematics to discover that light bends when it passes near massive objects, such as stars. This is due to the immense gravity of the objects. He also made observations about the photoelectric effect or the electrical effects due to the interaction of radiation (light) with matter.

FAMOUS FIRSTS

LIGHT THROUGH NOTHING
Scientists long believed that light could not travel through emptiness. It had to go through something. So the idea arose of an invisible substance called ether, which was everywhere — even in space. In 1887, Albert Michelson and Edward Morley used the interference of light (see page 41) to detect ether. They could not detect it, and the idea of ether was disproved.

The Michelson-Morley experiment used light beams that crossed back and forth over a huge slab of concrete.

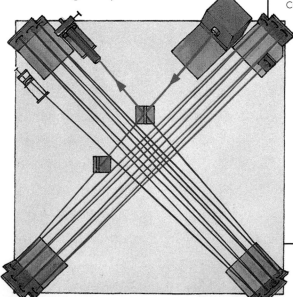

LASER LIGHT
The first laser was made in 1960 by Theodore Maiman. Lasers work when units of light called **photons** strike atoms that have excess energy. This creates more photons, and so on and so on, in a chain reaction. The light from a laser is all the same wavelength, and all the waves are in step or in phase. In contrast, ordinary light has a mixture of wavelengths and phases.

American scientist Theodore Maiman (1927-) constructed the first working laser from a ruby crystal that emitted red light.

Laser beams pierce the darkness and swish across the sky in spectacular light shows.

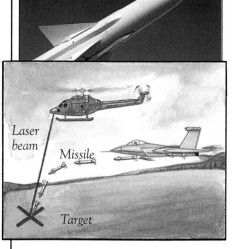

Laser beam

Missile

Target

Laser-guided missiles home in on a laser beam that shines from an aircraft. The missiles follow the laser to the target.

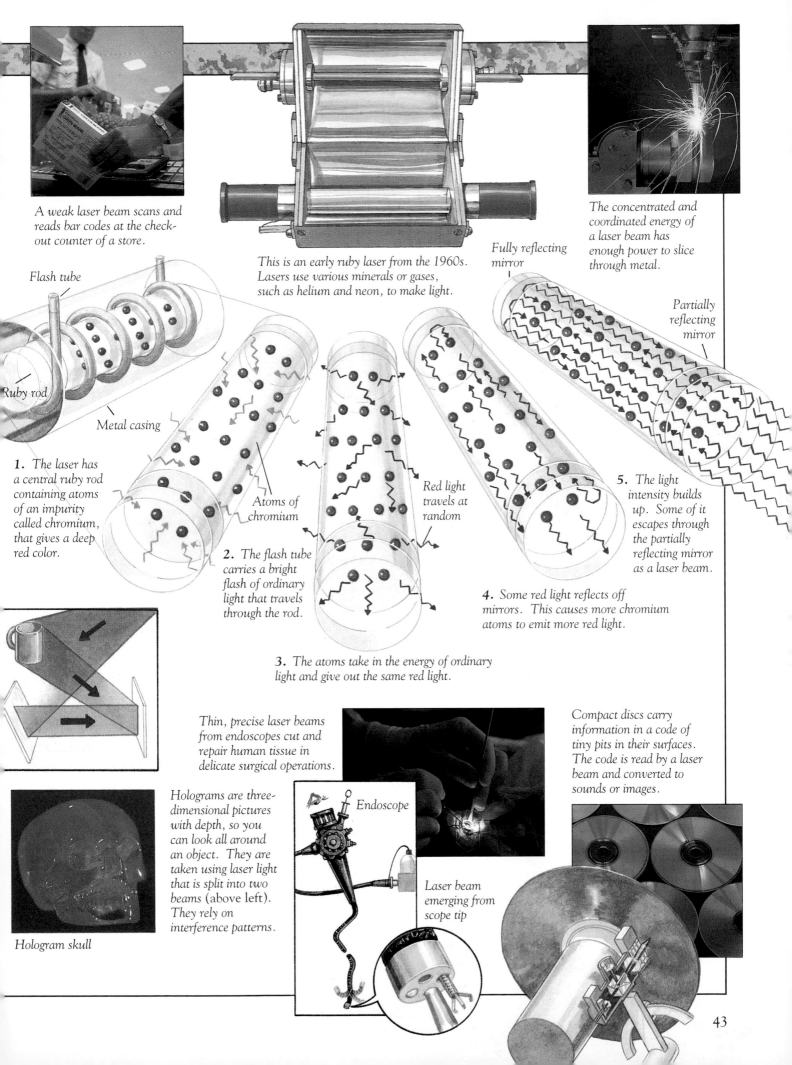

A weak laser beam scans and reads bar codes at the check-out counter of a store.

This is an early ruby laser from the 1960s. Lasers use various minerals or gases, such as helium and neon, to make light.

The concentrated and coordinated energy of a laser beam has enough power to slice through metal.

Flash tube

Ruby rod

Metal casing

Fully reflecting mirror

Partially reflecting mirror

1. The laser has a central ruby rod containing atoms of an impurity called chromium, that gives a deep red color.

Atoms of chromium

Red light travels at random

2. The flash tube carries a bright flash of ordinary light that travels through the rod.

3. The atoms take in the energy of ordinary light and give out the same red light.

4. Some red light reflects off mirrors. This causes more chromium atoms to emit more red light.

5. The light intensity builds up. Some of it escapes through the partially reflecting mirror as a laser beam.

Thin, precise laser beams from endoscopes cut and repair human tissue in delicate surgical operations.

Compact discs carry information in a code of tiny pits in their surfaces. The code is read by a laser beam and converted to sounds or images.

Holograms are three-dimensional pictures with depth, so you can look all around an object. They are taken using laser light that is split into two beams (above left). They rely on interference patterns.

Hologram skull

Endoscope

Laser beam emerging from scope tip

43

Newton supported the idea that light energy is in the form of tiny units called photons. In the nineteenth century, the idea of light as waves became more popular. Today, we can view light as being particles or waves. This double-view is called the "wave-particle duality" of light.

In the 1960s, the science of light entered a new era with the invention of the laser now used in surgery, telecommunications, and household goods. Researchers are also developing better photovoltaic (solar) cells (see page 23) that can produce useful amounts of electricity in low-light, overcast conditions as well as in bright sunlight. If these light-powered devices become available, they will serve to capture the "free" energy of sunlight and contribute greatly to solving the world's energy and environmental crises.

- Scientists aimed a laser beam at the Moon. It reflected back off a mirror placed there by a spacecraft. The complete journey took less than three seconds. The returning beam was as thin as a pencil.

Some homes have solar panels to help supply electricity.

Solar factories need very large areas to collect plenty of light.

- Solar cells are becoming more and more cost-effective.

FAMOUS FIRSTS

LIGHT TO STEER BY

Even in these days of computers, radio-tracking, and radar, lighthouses still provide a valuable service to ships. Their flashing beacons warn of dangers, such as rocky outcrops or sandbanks just below the surface. The first famous lighthouse was the Pharos Lighthouse of Alexandria, Egypt. It was the sixth of the Seven Ancient Wonders of the World. It was built in 280 B.C. but was destroyed by an earthquake in the thirteenth century.

To warn ships, a fire of wood or oil burned at the top of the Pharos Lighthouse, which was 400 feet (122 m) tall. The fire was reflected in polished metal mirrors, making it visible up to 31 miles (50 km).

The typical modern lighthouse has a very powerful electric lamp. This stays lighted, while lenses rotate around it to make the beam sweep in a circle and appear to "flash."

TALKING WITH LIGHT

When light travels from glass to air, it may be bent by refraction *(see page 30)*. But if it hits the surface at a shallower angle, the light reflects back into the glass, as if from a mirror. This is called total internal reflection. It is the principle behind fiber-optic communications, where sounds or any other type of information are coded as pulses of laser light.

Laser light travels along the fiber, even if it is bent, by reflecting repeatedly in short, straight lines.

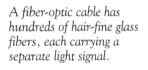

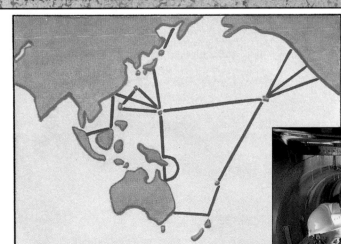

A fiber-optic cable has hundreds of hair-fine glass fibers, each carrying a separate light signal.

Between all of them, the optical fibers transmit an entire scene.

You can show the principle of total internal reflection using water instead of glass.

You need
Large plastic bottle, water, scissors, powerful flashlight, darkened conditions.

1. Carefully pierce a small hole in the side of the bottle. Put the bottle in a sink or tray in a dark place. Fill it with water, and shine a flashlight as shown.

2. The water spurts from the bottle. The light from the flashlight should travel along the stream of water by total internal reflection, like laser light along an optical fiber. Put your finger in the water to see the beam.

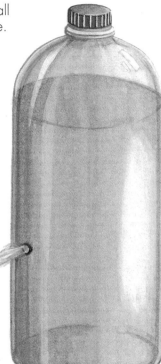

Fiber-optic cables were laid across the Atlantic Ocean in 1989 and the Pacific Ocean in 1990.

- Many telephone lines carry information, not as electrical signals along a wire, but as pulses of light along an optical fiber.

- Light carries signals along optical cables about 30 percent faster than electricity carries signals along metal wires.

- As you talk on the telephone, the sounds in your voice are changed to electricity, and then to codes of laser light pulses that flash at over 45 million times each second!

When compared to metal electrical cables, fiber-optic cables are light and flexible.

GLOSSARY

atom — the smallest part of an element that can exist by itself or in combination with other atoms.

bioluminescence — the emission of light from living things.

chlorophyll — a green substance in plants that absorbs the energy found in sunlight and turns it into energy-rich food.

concave — curved inward like the inside surface of a spoon.

constellation — a pattern or group of stars.

convex — curved outward like the outer surface of a spoon.

filament — a very thin wire.

fluorescent — a type of lighting that uses a glass tube containing a mixture of vapors, especially mercury vapor. Electricity is passed over the vapor, making the vapor glow.

kaleidoscope — an optical toy in which the reflection of objects in one mirror is itself reflected in another mirror.

lens — a clear material, such as glass, that is curved in order to bend light rays.

mirage — an optical illusion in which an object appears to be visible in the distance, but it does not actually exist.

nuclear fusion — the process in which four atoms of hydrogen join to produce one atom of helium. This fusion gives off light, heat, and other forms of energy.

optics — the science and study of light.

periscope — a scientific instrument that uses reflections from two mirrors to see over the top of or around the side of an object.

phosphorescence — a process by which objects glow in the dark.

photon — a unit of intensity of light.

photosynthesis — a process in which plants use energy from the Sun to make food.

polarized — a condition when waves are vibrating in a definite pattern in the same direction.

prism — a piece of glass, a raindrop, or another transparent material that refracts light into the colors of the rainbow.

refracted — bent or reflected from a straight path.

retina — a lining on the inside of the eye that is sensitive to light and is connected to the brain.

right angle — the angle at the corner of a square or rectangle.

spectrum — the rainbow of colors that become visible when light is broken up by a prism.

translucent — a feature of a substance that permits the passage of light, but the light is scattered.

transparent — a feature of a substance that permits the passage of light without scattering the light.

undulating — flowing in waves.

WEB SITES

www.earthsky.com/./1996/es960313.html

www.deltatech.com/deltatech/rainbowx.html

seds.lpl.arizona.edu/nineplanets/nineplanets/sol.html

tbci.org/~allisonh/bio.html

www.nosc.mil/planet_earth/optics.html

www.optics.org/optosigma/prisms/prisms.html

BOOKS

Hands on Science (series). (Gareth Stevens)

Kids Can! (series). *The Kids' Science Book.*
Robert Hirschfeld (Gareth Stevens)

Lasers: The New Technology of Light.
Charlene W. Billings (Facts on File)

Light. Neil Ardley (Simon and Schuster)

Light Action: Amazing Experiments with Optics.
Vicki Cobb and Joshua Cobb (HarperCollins)

Light and Color. Frank Millson (Troll)

Light and Illusions. Alan Ward (Chelsea House)

Light and Shadow. T. Davis Bunn (Chariot)

Light in Space. Wendy Orr (Firefly)

Microscope. Stwertka (Silver Burdett)

Photosynthesis. Herbert Y. Nakatan
(Carolina Biological)

Prisms. Mark Dunster (Linden)

Rainbows, Mirages, and Sundogs. Roy A. Gallant
(Simon and Schuster Children's)

Record Breakers (series). *Machines and Inventions.*
Peter Lafferty (Gareth Stevens)

Simple Science Projects (series): *Projects with Color
and Light.* John Williams (Gareth Stevens)

Sir Isaac Newton. Deborah Hitzeroth and Sharon
Leon (Lucent)

Telescope: Searching the Heavens.
Deborah Hitzeroth (Lucent)

VIDEOS

The Electromagnetic Spectrum and Vision.
(Benchmark Media)

Energy Alternatives: Solar. (Films for the
Humanities and Sciences)

Exploring the Spectrum. (Natural Energy Works)

Frontiers of Microscopy. (Films for the Humanities
and Sciences)

How a Photograph Is Made. (Films for the
Humanities and Sciences)

How Do Lenses Work? (Encyclopædia Britannica
Educational Corporation)

How to Bend Light. (Encyclopædia Britannica
Educational Corporation)

How Does Light Travel? (Encyclopædia Britannica
Educational Corporation)

How Plants Get Food. (MBG Videos)

How Plants Grow. (MBG Videos)

PLACES TO VISIT

George Eastman House
International Museum of Photography and Film
900 East Avenue
Rochester, NY 14607

California Academy of Sciences
Golden Gate Park
San Francisco, CA 94118

Ontario Science Center
770 Don Mills Road
Don Mills, Ontario M3C 1T3

Inventure Place
National Inventors Hall of Fame
221 South Broadway Street
Akron, OH 44308-1505

INDEX